THE GREAT LEAP WESTWARD

J.B. Caverty and Torrey Maloof

Consultants

Vanessa Ann Gunther, Ph.D.
Department of History
Chapman University

Nicholas Baker, Ed.D.
Supervisor of Curriculum and Instruction
Colonial School District, DE

Katie Blomquist, Ed.S.
Fairfax County Public Schools

Publishing Credits

Rachelle Cracchiolo, M.S.Ed., *Publisher*
Conni Medina, M.A.Ed., *Managing Editor*
Emily R. Smith, M.A.Ed., *Series Developer*
Diana Kenney, M.A.Ed., NBCT, *Content Director*
Courtney Patterson, *Senior Graphic Designer*
Lynette Ordoñez, *Editor*

Image Credits: Cover and p. 1 Washington University, St. Louis, USA/Bridgeman Images; pp. 3, 17, 26 Granger, NYC; pp. 11, 14-15 Sarin Images/Granger, NYC; pp. 4, 9, 16, 19, 31 North Wind Picture Archives; p. 5 American Museum of Western Art - The Anschutz Collection, Denver, Colorado, USA/Bridgeman Images; p. 7 Service Historique de la Marine, Vincennes, France/Bridgeman Images; p. 12 (left) Everett Collection/ Newscom, (right) World History Archive/Newscom; p. 14 NARA [306420]; pp. 20-21 Battle of San Jacinto: Accession ID: CHA 1989.080; Courtesy State Preservation Board, Austin, TX; Original Artist: McArdle, Henry A. / 1836-1908; Photographer: Perry Huston, 8/3/94, post conservation.; p. 22 Wikimedia Commons/Public Domain; p. 27 (top) LOC [LC-DIG-ppmsca-09855], (bottom) Public Domain; p. 28 Bridgeman Images; p. 32 LOC [LC-DIG-ppmsca-09855]; all other images from iStock and/or Shutterstock.'

Library of Congress Cataloging-in-Publication Data

Names: J.B. Caverty, author.
Title: The great leap westward / J.B. Caverty.
Description: Huntington Beach, CA : Teacher Created Materials, [2017] |
Audience: Grades 4 to 6. | Includes index.
Identifiers: LCCN 2016034134 (print) | LCCN 2016038167 (ebook) | ISBN
9781493837915 (paperback) | ISBN 9781480757561 (eBook)
Subjects: LCSH: United States--Territorial expansion--Juvenile literature. |
Frontier and pioneer life--United States--Juvenile literature. | Frontier
and pioneer life--West (U.S.)--Juvenile literature. | West (U.S.)--Discovery and exploration--Juvenile literature. | West (U.S.)--History--To 1848--Juvenile literature. | West (U.S.)--History--1848-1860--Juvenile literature.
Classification: LCC E179.5 .R525 2017 (print) | LCC E179.5 (ebook) | DDC
978/.01--dc23
LC record available at https://lccn.loc.gov/2016034134

Teacher Created Materials
5301 Oceanus Drive
Huntington Beach, CA 92649-1030
http://www.tcmpub.com

ISBN 978-1-4938-3791-5

Table of Contents

The Growing Nation

"I was constantly exposed to danger and death." This is how Daniel Boone described the land near the Ohio River in the 1770s. That land would later become the state of Kentucky. Boone was a **frontiersman**. He was rugged and loved the wilderness. He risked life and limb to explore the West. In Boone's time, the western **frontier** was inhabited by many tribes. White **settlers** thought of it as a dangerous place. It is believed that Boone's stories are a mixture of both fact and fiction. Even so, they offer a glimpse into what life was like on the frontier.

When the United States began, there were just 13 states. By 1800, there were only 16 states. All of them were located in one thin strip of land in the East. But in the next 70 years, the United States tripled in size! It stretched into the great frontier that Boone described. How did this happen? One step at a time!

FACT OR FICTION?

Over time, Daniel Boone became an American folk hero. His adventurous tales of peril on the frontier captured the hearts of many. Whether fact or fiction, Boone's stories increased the nation's thirst for expansion.

Daniel Boone (pointing) and other frontiersmen

Big Purchase

The United States acquired new land whatever way it could. Sometimes, land was won in wars. Other times, it was taken by force. There were times that political deals were made. And there were times when the government simply bought land. This is what happened with the Louisiana Purchase.

DON'T GET CONFUSED!

When people think of the Louisiana Territory, they sometimes think of the state of Louisiana. But, the territory was much bigger than just the one state. The land eventually made up all or part of 15 different states!

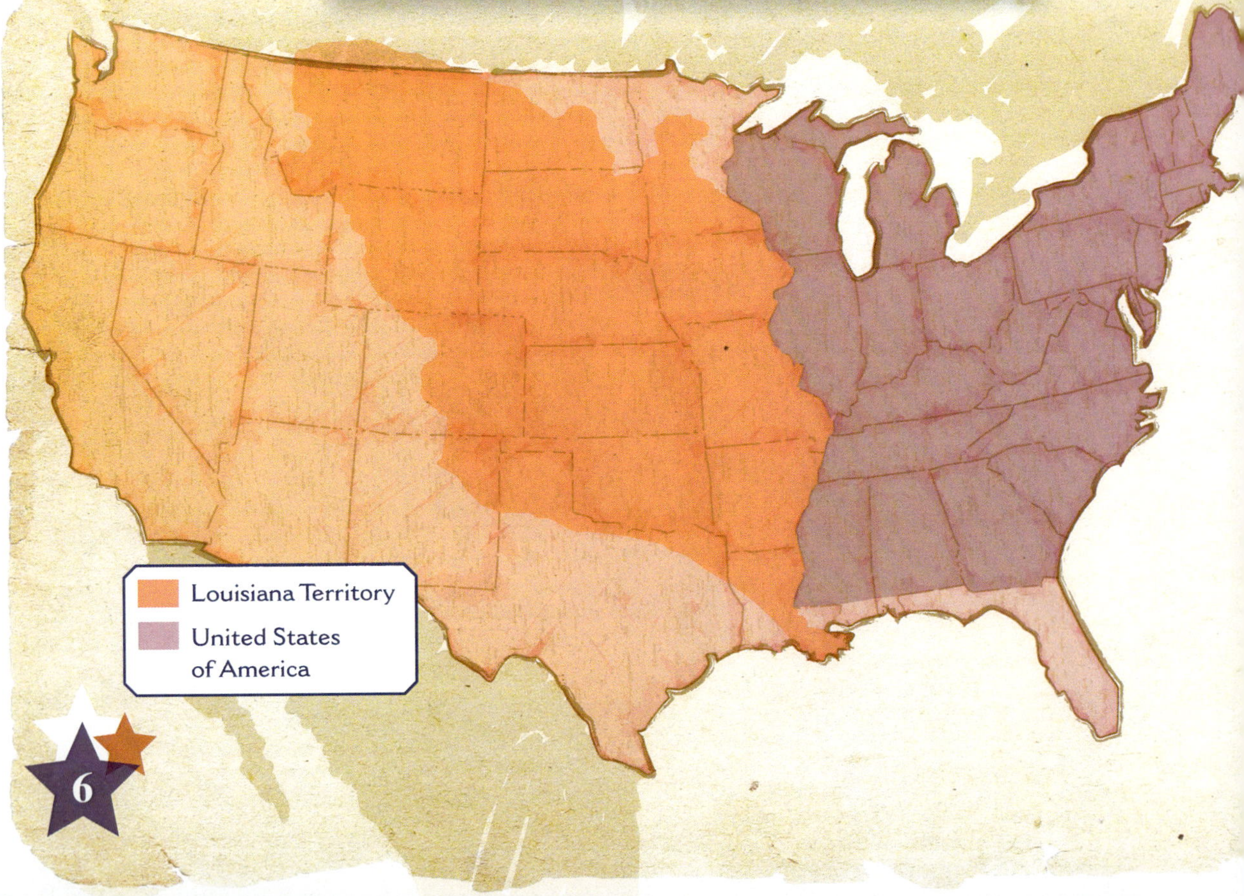

French explorers speak with an American Indian tribe.

Long before the United States was its own country, a group of French explorers came to the **continent**. They wanted to explore the **New World**. In 1682, they claimed a huge area of land. It started at the Gulf of Mexico and spread far to the North. The French named the land Louisiana after their king, Louis XIV.

Louis XIV

Back then, people did not think the big stretch of land was worth much. As such, the king of France gave Louisiana to Spain. Spain had helped France in the Seven Years' War with Great Britain. But in 1800, Napoleon Bonaparte (BOH-nuh-part), the new leader of France, traded other land in Europe with Spain to regain Louisiana. France wanted to control land in North America again.

When France regained control of Louisiana, it made many Americans angry. Spain had agreed to let Americans use the Mississippi River for three years. But when the **treaty** ran out, France did not renew it. The river was vital. Many traders used the river to send goods to the South. Without the river, they would have a difficult time transporting their goods. France also said that Americans could not store their goods in New Orleans. This was an important city. It had the busiest **port**!

In 1801, Thomas Jefferson became president. He was worried. He thought France would send soldiers to Louisiana. He didn't want to go to war with France. So, he came up with an idea.

A POWERFUL LEADER

Napoleon Bonaparte was a **dictator**. He ruled with total authority. Napoleon wanted to take over the entire world. But in the end, he pushed his soldiers too far. By 1814, his army was defeated.

Napoleon Bonaparte

A steamboat loaded with bales of cotton travels down a river.

Jefferson Makes a Deal

Jefferson believed he could solve the United States' problem with France if he bought New Orleans. So, he sent two **diplomats** to France to **negotiate** a deal. When the men arrived, they were met with a surprise. Not only was France willing to sell New Orleans, it wanted to sell the whole Louisiana Territory!

At first, the men did not know what to do. They had no way of reaching the president. Should they make a deal? Was it okay to buy that much land? They offered France $8 million. France said it wanted $15 million. After some talking, the Americans agreed. On May 2, 1803, they signed the Louisiana Purchase.

Jefferson was thrilled. The United States had just doubled in size! He sent Meriwether Lewis and William Clark to explore the new land. They traveled with their team all the way to the Pacific Ocean. When they returned, they shared everything they saw. They taught Americans about the new land out west.

Lewis and Clark expedition

Diplomats negotiate the Louisiana Purchase in France.

WHY SELL EVERYTHING?

Napoleon had two major reasons for selling all the land. He needed money to fight his wars. He also didn't want Americans to side with the British against France.

Big Announcement

Spain controlled many of the lands south of the United States. The Spanish had conquered present-day Mexico and large parts of Central and South America. But by 1821, most of these countries had gained their independence. Americans wanted to trade with these new nations and help them. They knew how hard it was to start a new country.

The British also wanted to trade with these new countries. But they were afraid that other European nations would try to take control of the region. If that happened, the British would not be able to trade. In 1823, British leaders wrote a letter to the United States. It said that the two countries should join together. They hoped this would warn other countries not to get involved.

James Monroe was president at the time. He spoke with many leaders and asked for advice. Thomas Jefferson and James Madison liked the British plan. But, John Quincy Adams was not so sure. He thought the United States should have its own policy without the British. After hearing these points of view, Monroe came up with his own plan.

James Monroe

John Quincy Adams

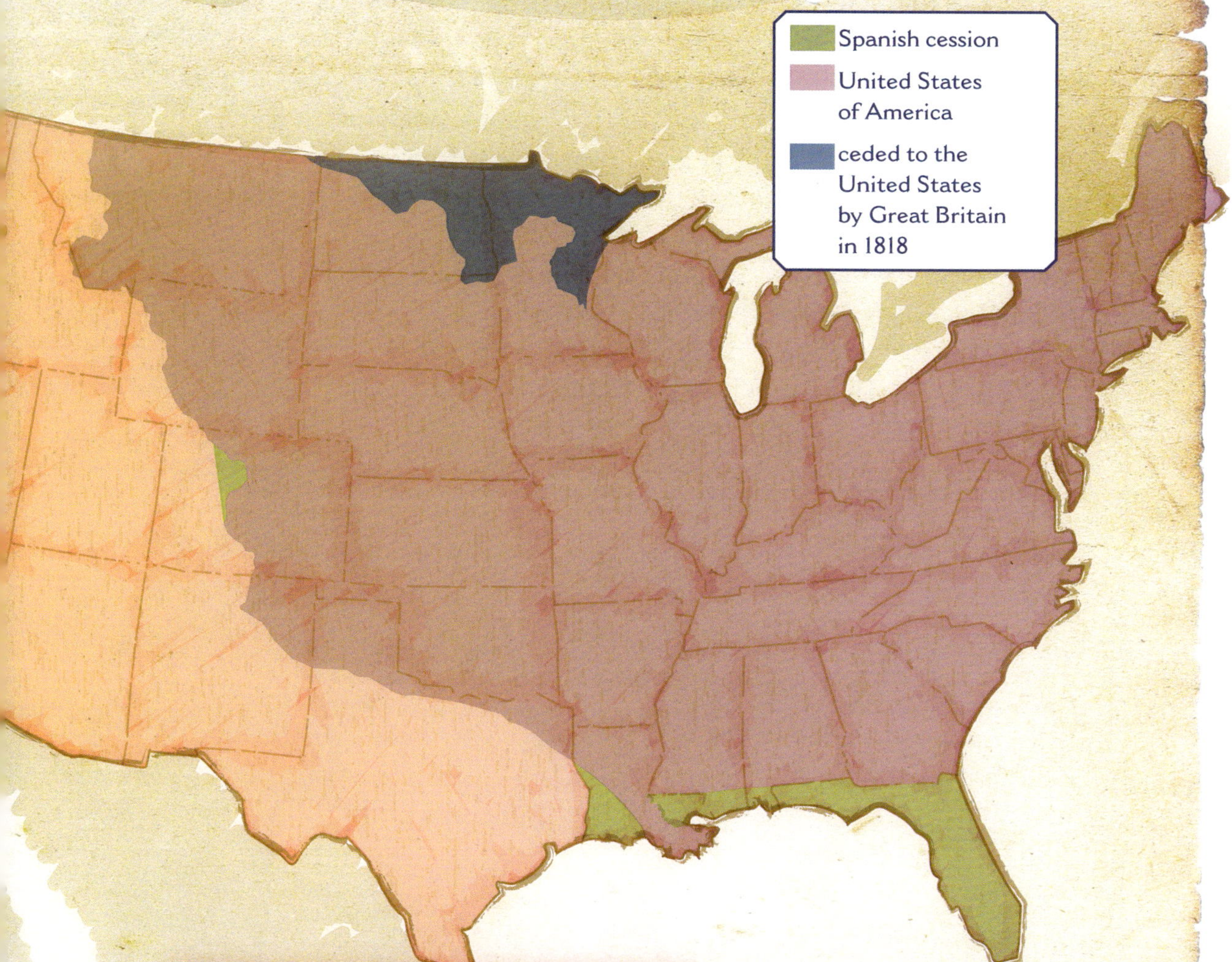

FLORIDA TERRITORY

The Florida Territory changed hands many times. Spain owned it for 250 years. Then, it went to Great Britain in 1763. Spain regained control in 1784. Then, Americans moved to Florida and claimed land. Since Spain was busy with other wars, it **ceded** Florida to the United States in 1821 with the Adams-Onís Treaty.

Monroe made his own announcement. It was a big one. He had a new, bold policy that came to be known as the Monroe **Doctrine**. It had four main points. First, it said that the United States would not get involved in European affairs. Next, it said that the United States would not interfere with existing New World colonies. It also said that the New World was closed to future colonization. Finally, it said that if any European country tried to control a New World nation, it would be seen as a threat to the United States. This was a big statement for a young country to make.

1.

Fellow Citizens of the Senate and House of Representatives.

Many important subjects will claim your attention, during the present Session, of which I shall endeavour to give, in aid of your deliberations, a just idea in this communication. I undertake this duty with diffidence, from the vast extent of the interests on which I have to tre[illegible] their great importance to every [illegible] our Union. I enter on it with zeal, from a thorough conviction, that there never was a period, since the establishment of our Revolution, when regarding the condition of the civilized world, and its bearing on us there was greater necessity for devotion in the public servants, to their respective duties, [illegible] and union, in

Monroe Doctrine

Monroe said that the United States had stayed out of European affairs. It had not joined wars in the past. It only joined in when American rights and freedoms were threatened. He felt this was a good policy and said it would continue. With this, the United States was telling the world that it could protect itself. It could also protect its neighbors. The Doctrine became the foundation for how the United States would deal with other nations. It would be used and cited for years to come.

James Monroe and other leaders discuss the Monroe Doctrine.

POWERFUL PRINCIPLES

Most European nations didn't pay attention to the Monroe Doctrine. But over time, it became one of the most important documents in American history. Many presidents after Monroe cited the principals stated in the Monroe Doctrine, including James Polk, Grover Cleveland, Theodore Roosevelt, Woodrow Wilson, John F. Kennedy, and Ronald Reagan.

Texas Territory

The Texas Territory changed hands many times. Spain and France both claimed land there. In 1821, the people living in the area won their freedom from Spain. They started a new nation called Mexico. At that time, Mexico was bigger than the United States.

Even so, Mexico needed help. More people were needed in the northern part of the country. This area was known as Tejas (TAY-has), or Texas. Leaders of the Mexican government wanted people to settle the land. They also hoped these people would help defend the new nation. So, they invited Americans to move to Texas. Thousands of them poured in. They liked the idea of new land. They thought they could make money there. Many thought it would be an adventure. By the 1830s, there were more Americans than Mexicans in Texas. This started to cause big problems when Santa Anna became president in 1832.

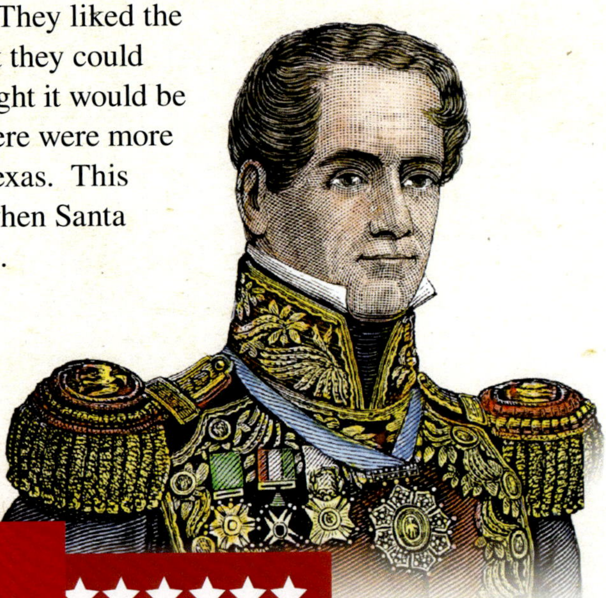

MEET THE PRESIDENT

In 1832, Antonio López de Santa Anna became president of Mexico. He was a brutal ruler who handed out harsh punishments and gave himself a lot of power. Santa Anna called himself the Napoleon of the West. He made many Americans nervous.

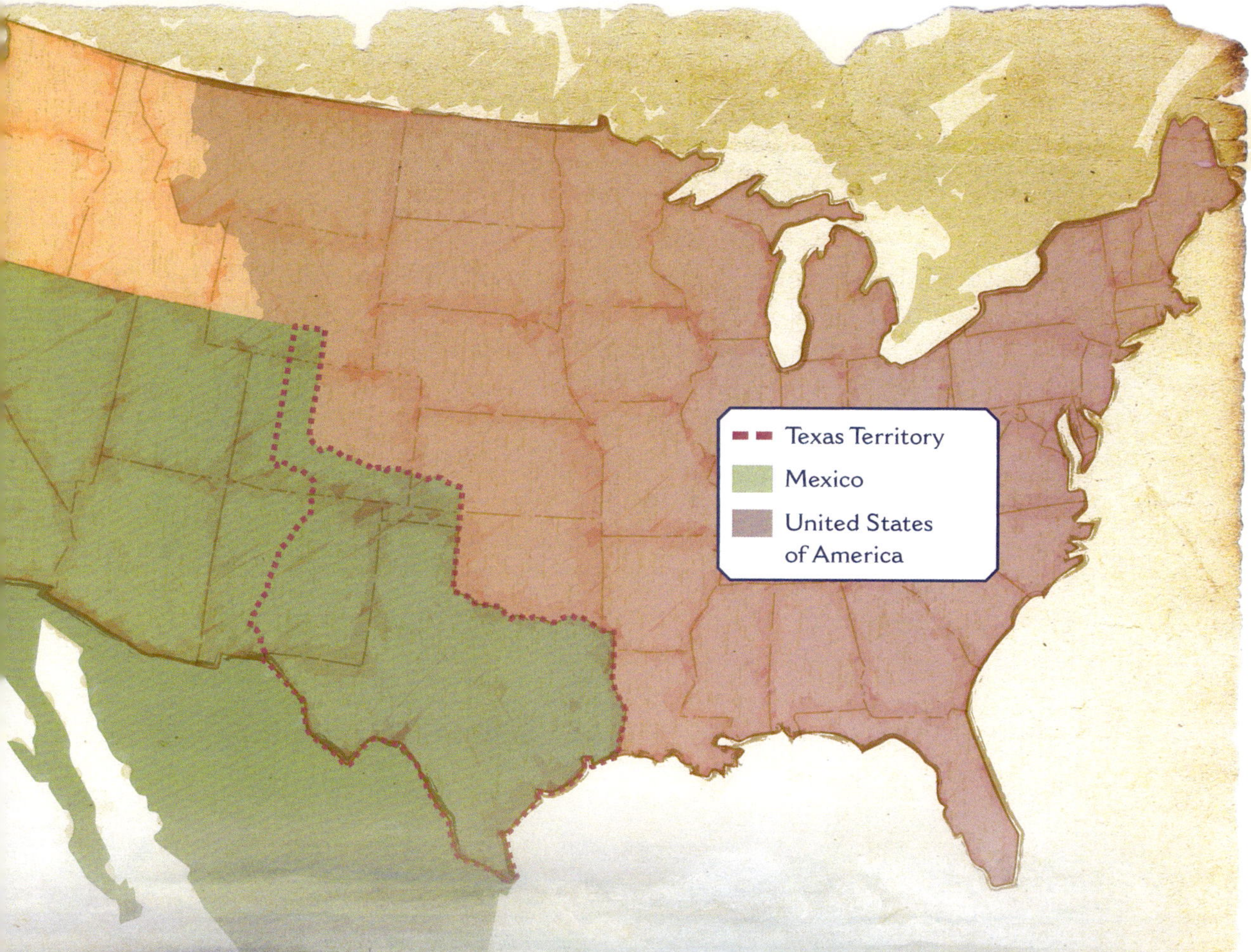

Settlers head west to claim new land.

Texas Revolution

Mexican leaders expected Texans to follow their laws. First, they had to become Mexican citizens. Next, they had to become **Catholic**. Lastly, they were not allowed to own slaves. But, many Texans did not obey these rules. This angered Santa Anna.

In 1836, Texans said they no longer wanted to be part of Mexico. They would start a new country called the Republic of Texas. When Santa Anna heard the news, he sent soldiers. In San Antonio, 7,000 Mexican soldiers surrounded a **fort** called the Alamo. Inside was a group of about 180 Texans. There were men, women, and children. The Texans knew they were outnumbered. Yet, they refused to give up. They held strong for 13 days. But, on March 6, they ran out of **ammunition**. The Mexicans stormed the fort, killing almost everyone inside. Less than 20 people survived. The Alamo had fallen. But, the war was not over.

the Alamo today

Mexican soldiers attack the Alamo.

REMEMBER THE ALAMO

Texans were angry about what took place at the Alamo. They thought the Mexicans should have taken prisoners instead of killing all the men. Texan soldiers started saying, "Remember the Alamo!" to inspire them to fight.

The Battle of the Alamo inspired Texans. They refused to give up. They kept fighting for their independence. A man named Sam Houston led 800 Texan soldiers into battle. On April 21, 1836, they reached the city of San Jacinto (SAN ha-SEEN-toe). About 1,200 Mexican soldiers were resting there. Houston and his men attacked. In less than 20 minutes, they captured or killed all the soldiers. They also caught Santa Anna. They took him prisoner. He agreed to give Texas its independence if they would spare his life. The Texans took the deal. This ended the Texas Revolution.

Battle of San Jacinto

Mexican-American War

After the war, the two sides argued. They could not agree on the border. Mexicans said the border was the Nueces River. The Texans said they owned the land all the way to the Rio Grande. This border would make Texas twice as big! When it came time to make Texas a state, tensions peaked.

TEXAS STATE?

Texan leaders wanted their independence. But, they hoped that if they joined the United States, the U.S. Army would protect them from more disputes with Mexico. In 1845, Texan President Anson Jones stepped down so Texas could become a state.

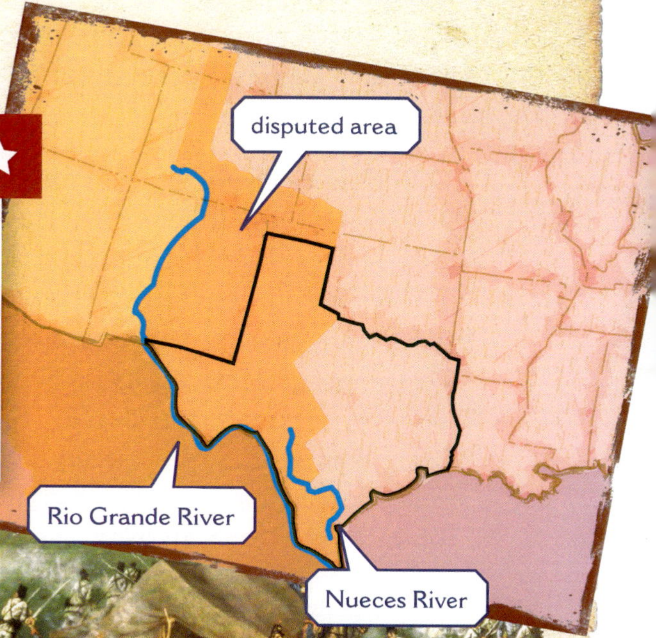

In 1845, President James K. Polk tried to buy the Southwest from Mexico, but Mexico refused. So, Polk sent soldiers to Texas. They marched to the area near the Rio Grande. They believed it was part of the United States, but the Mexicans said they owned it. Soon, a fight broke out. Some American soldiers were killed. Polk went to Congress and said that Mexicans had killed the soldiers "on American soil." This was not really true, since Mexicans claimed this land belonged to them. But, it worked. Congress declared war on Mexico in May of 1846.

James K. Polk

Both sides fought in Texas for months. In 1847, Polk sent troops farther south. He wanted them to take Mexico City. He thought that taking the capital was the only way to convince Mexico to give up the fight. After many months, U.S. troops reached the capital. They attacked Mexico City on September 14. The next day, Mexico **surrendered**. The war was over. Later, both sides signed a treaty. The United States agreed to pay Mexico $15 million for the land. Texas, all the way to the Rio Grande, was now part of the United States. Mexico also ceded more land to the United States. The growing country now stretched to the Pacific Ocean.

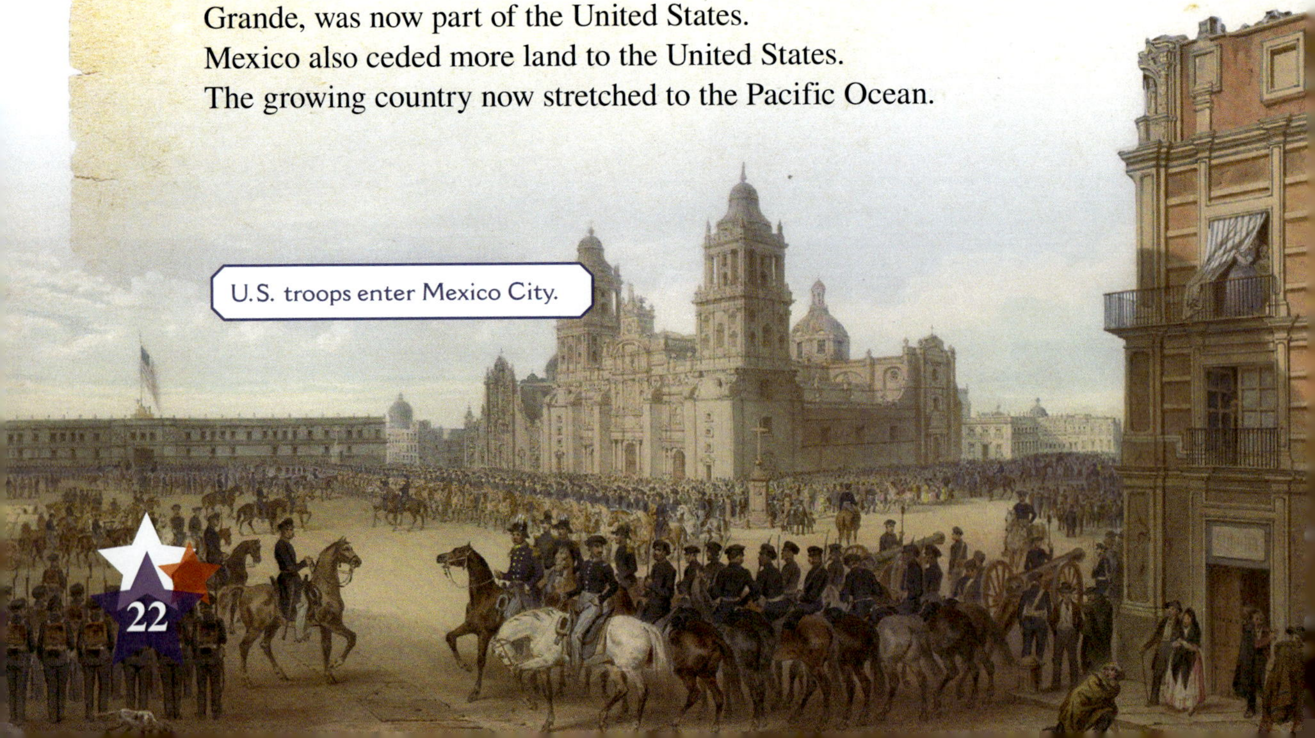

U.S. troops enter Mexico City.

OREGON TERRITORY

Meanwhile, in the Northeast, there was debate over who owned the Oregon Territory. In 1818, Great Britain and the United States agreed to share the land. But, this system did not work well. So, in 1846, both countries agreed that the land below the **49th parallel** was part of the United States.

THE GADSDEN PURCHASE

In 1853, James Gadsden went to Mexico and asked if the United States could buy some land for a railroad. Mexico needed money, so its leaders agreed. Mexico sold the land for $10 million.

Last Frontier

By the 1860s, the United States stretched from ocean to ocean. It seemed to have grown as much as it could. But, there was one last frontier that the United States wanted for its own.

The Alaska Territory was a huge stretch of land that Russia had controlled since the 1700s. Although big, for many years people thought the land had little value. It was cold and rugged. The weather was harsh. It was difficult to defend the land, too. Yet, Secretary of State William Seward wanted it. He wanted the nation to keep growing.

William Seward

After the Civil War, Seward worked out a deal. The United States would pay Russia \$7.2 million for the land. That's about 2¢ per acre. Russian leaders agreed. In 1867, the United States bought the land.

At first, people made fun of Seward's deal. They thought it was a waste of money. They called it Seward's **Folly**. But in 1896, gold was discovered in Alaska. The land had other **natural resources**, as well. There was coal and copper. There was oil and timber. Alaska turned out to be worth billions of dollars!

check from the U.S. Treasury for the purchase of Alaska

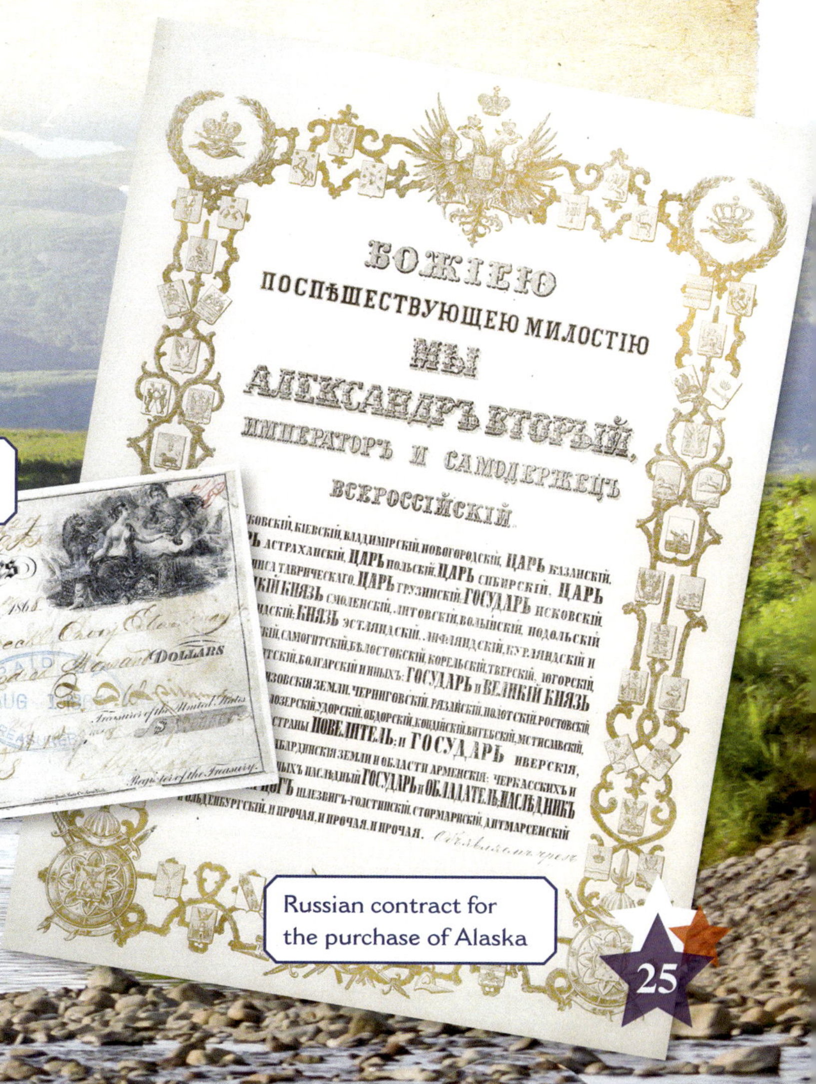
БОЖІЕЮ
ПОСПѢШЕСТВУЮЩЕЮ МИЛОСТІЮ
МЫ
АЛЕКСАНДРЪ ВТОРЫЙ,
ИМПЕРАТОРЪ И САМОДЕРЖЕЦЪ
ВСЕРОССІЙСКІЙ
...ковскій, Кіевскій, Владимірскій, Новогородскій, ЦАРЬ Казанскій,
...рь Астраханскій, ЦАРЬ Польскій, ЦАРЬ Сибирскій, ЦАРЬ
...нса Таврическаго, ЦАРЬ Грузинскій, ГОСУДАРЬ Псковскій
...кій КНЯЗЬ Смоленскій, Литовскій, Волынскій, Подольскій
...ндскій; КНЯЗЬ Эстляндскій, Лифляндскій, Курляндскій и
...кій, Самогитскій, Бѣлостокскій, Корельскій, Тверскій, Югорскій,
...тскій, Болгарскій и иныхъ; ГОСУДАРЬ и ВЕЛИКІЙ КНЯЗЬ
...зовскія земли, Черниговскій, Рязанскій, Полотскій, Ростовскій
...озерскій, Удорскій, Обдорскій, Кондійскій, Витебскій, Мстиславскій,
...страны ПОВЕЛИТЕЛЬ; и ГОСУДАРЬ Иверскія,
...бардинскія земли и области Арменскія: Черкасскихъ и
...ныхъ наслѣдный ГОСУДАРЬ и ОБЛАДАТЕЛЬ, НАСЛѢДНИКЪ
...цогъ Шлезвигъ-Голстинскій, Стормарнскій, Дитмарсенскій
...бургскій, и прочая, и прочая, и прочая.

Russian contract for the purchase of Alaska

Manifest Destiny

It is no shock that the United States grew after gaining its independence. What was shocking was how fast it grew. During the 1800s, expansion was rapid. Settlers moved west. New lands became states.

In 1845, westward expansion got another big push. A magazine editor named John O'Sullivan wrote an article about the country. He believed the United States was special. He said it had the God-given right to control the continent. He believed it was the nation's destiny. He called this idea Manifest Destiny. Some people disagreed with him. They thought it was wrong. After all, other people were already living in the West. But, many thought he was right. So did the leaders of the country. When O'Sullivan's article was written, there were only 27 states. By 1890, there were 42! The United States had started out as a small, new nation. But by the end of the 19th century, it was one of the largest and most powerful in the world. And it was all in the name of Manifest Destiny.

ANOTHER SIDE OF THE STORY

Manifest Destiny did not apply to African Americans or Asian Americans. Hispanics and women were left out, too. It resulted in American Indians being forced off their lands as shown in the image below. Today, Manifest Destiny is seen in a very different light than it was at the time.

This 1872 painting by John Gast shows Americans' attitudes about Manifest Destiny.

1839.] *The Great Nation of Futurity.* 427

his view over the past history of the monarchies and aristocracies of antiquity, and not deplore that they ever existed? What philanthropist can contemplate the oppressions, the cruelties, and injustice inflicted by them on the masses of mankind, and not turn with moral horror from the retrospect?

America is destined for better deeds. It is our unparalleled glory that we have no reminiscences of battle fields, but in defence of humanity, of the oppressed of all nations, of the rights of conscience, the rights of personal enfranchisement. Our annals describe no scenes of horrid carnage, where men were led on by hundreds of thousands to slay one another, dupes and victims to emperors, kings, nobles, demons in the human form called heroes. We have had patriots to defend our homes, our liberties, but no aspirants to crowns or thrones; nor have the American people suffered themselves to be led on by wicked ambition to depopulate the land, to spread desolation far and wide, that a human being might be placed on a seat of supremacy.

We have no interest in the scenes of antiquity, only as lessons of avoidance of nearly all their examples. The expansive future is our arena, and for our history. We are entering on its untrodden space, with the truths of God in our minds, beneficent objects in our hearts, and with a clear conscience unsullied by the past. ...

In this 1839 article, O'Sullivan writes about Manifest Destiny before he coined the term.

Vlog It!

Imagine you could travel back in time and live on a frontier discussed in this book. Which place would you choose? Would you explore the Louisiana Territory? Would you build a new town in Texas or Oregon? Or, maybe you'd rather brave the harsh elements of Alaska. Why would you choose that frontier? Create a video blog in which you explain your choice.

Glossary

49th parallel—the border that most of the United States falls south of, designating a line of latitude

ammunition—bullets and shells that are shot from weapons

Catholic—relating to the Roman Catholic Church

ceded—gave control of something to another group or government

continent—one of the seven large land masses of Earth

dictator—a person who rules a country with total authority and often in a cruel way

diplomats—people who represent their country's government while in another country

doctrine—a statement of government policy

folly—a foolish idea

fort—a strong building or place where soldiers live

frontier—an area where few people live

frontiersman—a man who lives in an area where few people live

natural resources—materials found in nature that can be used for economic gain

negotiate—formally discuss something in order to make an agreement

New World— the western hemisphere of the world; especially North, Central, and South America

port—a harbor where ships pick up and drop off goods

settlers—people who go to a new place to live

surrendered—agreed to stop fighting because you knew you would not win

treaty—a formal agreement made between two or more countries or groups

Index

Your Turn!

American Progress

The United States grew dramatically during the 1800s. People pushed west in search of new land and opportunities. Unfortunately, this was often at the expense of American Indians and other groups. John Gast painted this picture in 1872. He titled it *American Progress*. Carefully examine the people and the elements in this painting. The woman in the center represents the United States. How do you think Gast felt about Manifest Destiny? How do you think he felt about American settlers compared to American Indians? What point might he have tried to make with this painting? How do you know? Write a paragraph to explain your thinking.